Great Book of
Fairy
Patterns

by Lora S. Irish

Fox
Chapel Publishing

1970 Broad Street • East Petersburg, PA 17520
www.FoxChapelPublishing.com

Great Book of Fairy Patterns is an original work, first published in 2004 by Fox Chapel Publishing Company, Inc. The paintings/illustrations and patterns contained herein are copyrighted by the author. Readers may make three copies of these patterns for personal use. The patterns themselves, however, are not to be duplicated for resale or distribution under any circumstances. Any such copying is a violation of copyright law.

Publisher	Alan Giagnocavo
Book Editor	Ayleen Stellhorn
Editorial Assistant	Gretchen Bacon
Desktop Specialist	Linda Eberly
Cover Design	Jon Deck

ISBN 1–56523–225–9

To learn more about the other great books
from Fox Chapel Publishing, or to find a
retailer near you, call toll-free 1-800-457-9112
or visit us at **www.FoxChapelPublishing.com.**

Printed in China
10 9 8 7 6 5 4 3 2

Library of Congress Cataloging-in-Publication Data

Irish, Lora S.
        Great book of fairy patterns / by Lora S. Irish.
            p. cm.
        ISBN 1-56523-225-9 (pbk. Perfect bdg.: alk. paper)
        1. Handicraft 2. Fairies in art. I. Title.

    TT157.I74 2004
    745.5—dc22

                                                            2003069610

Dedication

This work is dedicated to two special, tiny Fairies, for they have graced my life with their love, laughter and charming antics: Andie Jane and Courtney. Although they now grace a flower garden in the midwestern prairies far from my home, they are forever in my heart. With love, from their Aunt Susie.

© Lora S. Irish

Acknowledgments

Special thanks go to Alan, Ayleen, Jon and everyone at Fox Chapel Publishing who worked on this project. Their encouragement and support throughout the creation of this book has been indispensable. It has, once again, been a delight for me to work with such a well-organized, creative team.

Table of Contents

Page 6   *Page 13*   *Page 15*

Page 19   *Page 29*   *Page 32*

From the Author and Artist

Growing up in a family full of craftsmen and artisans, I had no doubt that I would focus my attention on the arts. It seemed that there was always something being created in my childhood home. The dining room table was often full of newly cut quilt pieces, ceramic bisque and glazes, or plans for the most recent woodworking furniture endeavor. I can remember the pieces of an old muzzle-loading rifle submerged in a butter tub of oil, waiting for restoration, while the barrel hung from the patio door curtain rod coated with bluing and the gun stock sat ready to be woodcarved.

Arts and crafts filled my childhood home. Not hidden in some basement or workshop, all the creating seemed to happen right in the living room or dining room. Wonderful smells are associated with these memories: turpentine and linseed oil, cedar wood and walnut for carving, newly bought calico fabrics, and the makings for strawberry jelly on the stove.

Family get-togethers quickly turned into "show and tell" time as each uncle or aunt brought out his or her latest craftworks. My uncles brought photos of wood furniture, cabinetry work and welding projects. My aunts brought appliqué quilt tops, weaving projects fresh off the loom and petit point. Mom shared a variety of arts including knitting, oil painting and pictures of her latest prize-winning flower arrangement.

My house, just like my Mom's, is filled with art and craft supplies. A basket of cloth and thread sits on the floor next to my living room chair. The yarn ball basket rests across the room in the corner with needles and hooks ready for the next afghan to be started. My studio area is stuffed with boxes and totes full of paints, canvases and papers, glue, scissors and accessories.

When Fox Chapel offered me the opportunity to create the *Great Book of Fairy Patterns* it seemed to be the perfect format. It has been my experience that few artisans do just one craft or one style of art. Many of us enjoy a wide variety of creative endeavors. And many of us already have a strong understanding of our favorite art; all we really need are new ideas and patterns with which to express that art.

So, go grab your baskets, totes and boxes of art and craft supplies, and let's get started.

— Lora S. Irish

About the Author: Twelve of Lora S. Irish's purebred dog breed oil canvas paintings have been published as limited editions. She is the author of a series of woodcarving and craft pattern books including *Landscapes in Relief, Wildlife Carving in Relief, North American Wildlife Patterns for the Scroll Saw, World Wildlife Patterns for the Scroll Saw* and *The Great Book of Dragon Patterns.*

Working from their home studio, Lora and her husband and webmaster, Michael, are the owners of two internet websites: www.mut-tart.com and www.carvingpatterns.com. Their online art gallery, Fine Art Dog Prints, features the works of over 60 canine artists. Classic Carving Patterns is their internet woodcarving studio focusing on online tutorials, projects and patterns created exclusively by L. S. Irish for the crafter and artisan.

CHAPTER ONE

FAIRY ART

OR *How do I use this book in my artwork?*

F airies have become a popular and favorite theme for arts and crafts no matter what medium you use. A Flower Fairy in a field of daisies is a beautiful subject for tole painting, glass etching or ceramics. A Water Nymph is ideal for those who enjoy working with needle, thread and woven cloth in hand. If right now you are stretching paper for your next watercolor work, you may want to consider a Fairy with brightly colored dragonfly wings. Woodburners and woodcarvers might do well to consider a Forest Pixie to adorn a jewelry box or other work in progress. Maybe it's a Fairy that you want to adorn the pages of your newest photo scrapbook or to accent a set of scroll sawed garden stakes for your backyard flowerbed. A Fairy may just be the perfect idea for your next appliqué quilt or just the right image to add to your family Web site. The Fairy theme can be used to accent any arts or crafts project today.

I have designed the patterns in this book to be used with any number of arts and crafts projects. On the following pages you will see how I have altered patterns to include Fairies on wooden heart boxes, in a quilt block, on the pages of a scrapbook, in needlepoint and on canvas. The chapters in this book will teach you not how to do a particular art or craft but, instead, how to alter the patterns to fit your particular art or craft.

Bed of Petals, pattern on page 75

Acrylic paints are an excellent media
when painting fairies. These two designs,
Bed of Petals and *Pixie Perch*, are worked
over an acrylic-splatter basecoat on
papier-mâché boxes.

Pixie Perch, pattern on page 132

The Babysitter is done in oil paints over a stained wood background. This style of tole painting creates changing color tones in the wings, nest and blossoms of this design.

The Babysitter, pattern on page 108

Created with cotton fabric, a bias tape marker and a double-faced iron-on interfacing, this *Welsh Cattails* fairy has become the center panel of an appliqué quilt top.

Welsh Cattails, pattern on page 123

A Touch Daring is worked in watercolors on stretched paper. Watercolors offer the fairy artist a quick-and-easy method to create color combinations before starting a craft project.

A Touch Daring, pattern on page 73

© Lora S. Irish

Downy Perch, pattern on page 70

The pattern *Downy Perch* was transferred onto graph paper, and then charted to create this counted cross stitch.

Southern Charm, pattern on page 176

Scrapbooking seemed a perfect choice for *Southern Charm.* With pre-printed scrapbook paper, a glue stick and scissors, this fairy quickly became the accent for a photo album.

Hand-painted invitations not only inform your guests of the time of your party but also become wonderful artwork keepsakes.

© Lora S. Irish

You're Invited, pattern on page 109

CHAPTER TWO

A HISTORY OF FAIRIES IN LEGENDS

OR How did Fairies, Faes and Flutterbyes come to be?

A s an artist I have always believed that the first principle of creating any artwork is that the artist needs to clearly know and understand the subject that he is representing. Any subject that an artist renders deserves to be researched so that the final work truly is representative of the actual object, scene or story. Art is viewed as stories written in color, as visual tales with visual morals and visual truths. So to include errors in the subjects of our paintings because we did not take the time to learn about what we are creating passes on misinformation.

Over the last many months I have read countless folklore, and with each story, I have faithfully written down the descriptions provided by our ancestors. Fairy illustrations and paintings are plentiful, as they have captured the minds and hearts of artists for centuries. These wonderful bits of artwork and lore provide a wide range of descriptive information on our subject of Fairies, which are sometimes referred to as Faes and Flutterbyes.

It should be noted, in passing, that there are numerous stories called "Fairy tales," yet only a few of these refer directly to the race of the Fairy people. Under the category of literature called Fairy tales, you will find many different magical creatures and mythical races. These stories tell about brownies, elves and gnomes, talking sly foxes and wise ravens and ogres and spirits that live in the darkness. A few tell about our subject, the Fairy. So, reading a Fairy tale does not necessarily mean you will read about Fairies.

The oldest lore, circa 1100–1800

The best place to start any endeavor usually is at the beginning, so let's take a look at the earliest recorded Fairy stories. Some of the oldest tales directly referring to a race or species of small human-like beings called Fairies date back to the 1100s in the British Isles. Often these tales were passed down by word of mouth through the generations as families gathered in the evenings by the fire. A grandfather or aged uncle could mesmerize even the littlest in the house with stories of magical people who brought rewards to the worthy, meted out punishment to those that erred into sinful ways, and caused unexplainable occurrences in the daily lives of man. Over the centuries these tales were used as a way to record notable events in the community as well as to entertain.

The descriptions these tales give for Fairies are wide and change often depending on the story, the land in which the story first appeared and the time period. But general guidelines can be found.

Fairies have light hair the color of golden, dried wheat or strawberry red locks with tight ringlets surrounding their faces. Bright, laughing blue eyes often accent their rosy, red cheeks. However, Fairies also can be dark and sultry, full of mischief and revenge, with black, straight hair surrounding a craggy face with deep-set, dark eyes.

The stories are clear in regards to Fairies' statures. They do not stand very tall, usually smaller than a toddler of two years down to the size of a man's thumb. Yet even with their diminutive size, Fairy maidens were sought after as wives for young men because of their alluring beauty and sweet voice. The small size seems to change when, on the night of a Fairy child's birth, the Fairy father rides up to the house of the local human midwife on a full-sized horse, large enough to carry both of them back to the palace to help deliver the baby. Usually this same Fairy father would be seen riding greyhounds that were specially bred for this purpose, not horses.

Colors abound when we read the old legends. A Fairy might be dressed in rags or in a queenly gown. Men were said to wear jackets of red and green. The ladies seem to have a fondness for brightly colored petticoats. Vibrantly colored clothing seems to be one constant in Fairy tales, except when it is time for a Fairy princess to give birth. At that moment the tales clearly state that she is dressed in a shade of white so pure it shimmers with opulence and that all who attend her are dressed in the same manner.

The singing voice of a Fairy is magical and can lure an unsuspecting man deep into the Fairy rings of dance where he is destined to dance for years and years. Lulled by the captivating tunes, the mortal man feels his troubles and fears seemingly disappear, which eases him through the day's toils or compels him to follow the beautiful voice into unexpected adventures.

Fairies seem to be shy and elusive, yet when they are seen they can change the life of any human. A poor and starving farmer who grants just a tiny favor to a Fairy can find he now is gifted a magical cow that gives so much milk it fills every pail offered. A man who bears the weight of the world on his shoulders and responsibilities far beyond his means because of a lazy and demanding wife can find himself rescued to a Fairy palace of wealth and luxury. For the courtesy of a pan of warm water for bathing, a small pile of straw by the hearth for sleeping and a bit of bread crumbs for eating, a Fairy will leave an old woman's home sparkling clean with a small silver coin on her table.

Fairies, however, are not above mischief and revenge. A Fairy will cast a spell upon the coin that she leaves on the hearth, so if the old woman ever tells of the Fairy's visit, the coin will turn to black dust. If you anger a Fairy, you could find that your favored daughter is lured into a Fairy palace, destined to be held as a captive until her wedding day is years past. One little vixen was especially known for letting the cattle out of their stalls just so she could hear the animals' wondrous cowbells

The Gathering, pattern on page 141

Laundry Line Gossip, pattern on page 164

ring when they walked.

Every story agrees that Fairies are people of the night. Coming out from their homes beside an old tree, a small cave or a deeply cut riverbank, the Fairies are active until the rising of the sun. They are seldom seen during the daytime unless they need to visit the marketplace. Here they go about their business, dropping a few coins at the bread maker's table and taking the freshest of loaves, with not a word said.

As Fairies do not seem to work at any occupation, neither tilling the land nor herding beasts, it must be assumed that Fairy money is magical in its origins. This assumption seems to hold true as one story tells of a pocketful of silver Fairy coins that a boy received from a Fairy in exchange for the family's prized cow. The coins then turned into a handful of corn when brought home to his mother and father.

Of note in trying to describe Fairies, it is agreed that Fairies hate lying and sworn oaths of any kind. One man lied to a Fairy and incurred such wrath that the Fairy folk tormented not only him but also his offspring for many generations hence. For a Fairy to take an oath was considered foolishness as it bound the Fairy to one place and one person, contrary to his free-spirited nature. However, Fairies always seemed to bind humans to contracts in exchange for little magical gifts. If you broke the contract, even by an accident that you did not cause, the gift and all that it had touched or affected would disappear.

The status of Fairies ranges from the very poorest, who appears as a goose herder in an early version of the Cinderella story called Tattercoat, to the beautiful kings and queens that reside in lavish palace caves. Yet whether beggars or princes, Fairies love to dance. Late in the evening the music from the Fairy ring can be heard as these little people dance for hours around their favorite oak, yew or sycamore tree, but never a rowan tree, for this was said to bring harm to the Wee Folk.

Recurring themes in the old tales

Just as you find different descriptions of Fairies in the oldest legends, you also find a wide variety of themes and story lines. Just about anything you could ever imagine can happen if one encounters a Fairy, and then the adventure would be told and retold until it became what we might today call an "urban legend."

There does seem to be a small handful of stories that appear to repeat and that are not bound to one particular location or time period. These are the Fairy tales that use the magic of the race to explain odd instances and unexpected occurrences in the lives of people. Several stories are excellent examples of this. Let's explore just a few to discover the basic idea behind the Fairy tale.

The Tale of the Fairy Ring Dance

A story that is often told revolves around the Fairy ring dance and is an old version of *Rip van Winkle* by Washington Irving. This story begins late at night as a man is walking along a wood-lined, deserted road. (Human women, for some unknown reason, do not appear in this particular story.) Suddenly he hears the sweet melody of the fiddle and the pipe coming from under a large tree just a short way from the roadbed. Curious and drawn by the lovely music, he creeps toward the tree to discover a band of Fairies dancing merrily around and around the tree's base. A lively Fairy maiden grabs the man's hand as she passes by him, encouraging him to join in the fun.

As the evening goes by, he abandons his hesitation and throws himself into the spirit of the evening, enjoying every twist and turn of the dance. When dawn's light creeps into the woods, the man is overcome with weariness and finally pulls himself away from the merriment to fall asleep on a bed of soft grass. Little does he know as he drifts off that it will be anywhere from one year and one day to five hundred years later when he awakes or that he will return to a human world that is strangely changed and unknown to him. When this poor soul does finally make it home, he discovers that everyone he has ever known has died, his house has been long sold, and there is no one who knows anything about him, except for a small piece of old gossip about the "man who never came home." Many of the variations of this story end with the man, now decrepitly old, turning to dust before the next sunset.

The main character of "The Tale of the Fairy Ring Dance" seems to fall into one of three types. The first character type is the overly responsible man. This gentleman finds himself doing more labors than he physically can stand as no one else— neither wife, nor children, nor grandchildren—will lend themselves to the work. He often is noted as having a demanding wife with a wicked tongue, who may have managed to create a large debt due to her spending well beyond his meager means.

The second type of man that shows up in the tale is the misunderstood son. These versions tell about a young man who, no matter how hard he works or applies himself to his lessons, can never accomplish as much as his sire expects of him. The boy will be noted as having struggled for years to earn even one small scrap of respect from his father. Though he will have achieved more than any other man of his age in the village, in his father's eyes he will always be a failure.

The third character type that appears in these stories is the chronic drunk. This version usually begins with noting that the man is, once again (since it is a regular practice), returning home from the village tavern after a hard evening of drinking. It is also noted in these stories that his wife, who is waiting at home, is ready to once again deliver a firm tongue-lashing in response to his drunken state.

It would be a major topic of gossip in any small village if one day a man disappeared, never to be seen nor heard from again in the lifetime of his family and friends. In reading the tales it seems that any of these men might have finally had enough of their rough lot in life and might have chosen to simply leave their homes and families in hopes of finding happiness somewhere else. The recurring story about the Fairy ring dances gives a reason for a man's disappearance from his home without laying blame on either his family or society.

The Tale of the Fairy Princess Wife

This story also concerns the human males of the time. Here the man is attending to his regular tasks of the day when he suddenly comes upon a beautiful, unknown woman. Often she is singing and her music entrances him and draws him to her. The woman, of course, is instantly identified as a Fairy princess. The gentleman, overcome with love, pleads with her to marry him. She refuses him, unless he can perform some small request. The request can be anything from telling her a story that makes her laugh to bringing her bread that is properly baked or presenting her with a special flower or charm. The man spends many days trying to please the Fairy princess, and finally he accomplishes his task well enough to win her heart.

At this point in the story, her father arrives and grants his permission for the man to marry his daughter. However, the father states that if the man should ever strike the Fairy princess with iron, the marriage will be ended. In this stipulation the father may indicate the number of blows that will end the marriage, anywhere from one to three, but does not indicate whether it makes any difference if the husband meant to strike the wife or if he strikes her by accident. Of note here is the Fairy's fear of anything made of this metal.

Three things are certain in the story. First, the man and the woman, deeply in love and devoted to each other, will enjoy a wonderful married life together. Second, there will be children born to the couple. Third, of course, is that the husband will somehow accidentally strike his wife with iron. Often it is a horse's bridle that hits her when the man and his wife are trying to saddle the animal.

At that moment when the iron strikes the Fairy princess, she disappears, never to be seen again. When she leaves, the stories tell us, she will abandon her husband and her children, but she will always take her dowry of magical cows with her.

The main character in this story is a man who somehow bears a social burden. He may be noted as being very old, ugly, simple or just plain mean. Had he not, by sheer chance, found a Fairy princess for a wife, he probably would never have married, for his social flaw implies that a human woman would have passed him over for a more suitable husband. The Fairy princess's choice of him as a husband is not based on the personality or on the appearance of the man but on the task that is to be performed. Therefore his social burden does not affect his acceptability as a marriage partner.

"The Tale of the Fairy Princess Wife" is another disappearance story; only this time it is the woman who does the disappearing. She has lived with her husband for some time, as she is often noted as having more than one child. The contract stated by the Fairy father gives some clue as to why this woman may have disappeared; it clearly refers to the striking or beating of the wife by the husband, a common event at the time. Sadly the true ending to this story may have been that the husband, in a fit of rage and after years of spousal abuse, killed her. If this were the case, it would also explain why the striking of the Fairy princess with iron was always an accident, as it would have been the husband who was left to tell his neighbors why his wife had disappeared. "The Tale of the Fairy Princess Wife" is used to explain how a wife might suddenly disappear without a trace.

In conducting research for this book, I did discover one variation of this story that caught my attention. This version of the tale begins by declaring the husband to be of a mean and cruel nature. He was so mean that everyone in the village knew that he beat his wife often and violently. Now it happened, while the husband and wife were plowing the fields one day, that the horse

Darwin Tulips, pattern on page 78

© Lora S. Irish

became unruly and the wife was unable to control the beast. Falling into a rage, the husband began to beat her. (Note here that she, not the horse, is the recipient of his violence.) This angered two passing Fairy men who had been watching the couple work the farm. They promptly picked up the husband and threw him into a lake. Although she pleaded desperately with them to return her poor husband, the Fairies told her firmly, "Into the lake we have put him and in the lake he will stay!" The story ends with the husband never being seen again, but the wife was noted as living happily ever after.

Magical cows

Now about those cows that the Fairy princess took with her in the story above…. Magical cows appear frequently throughout the ages. Magical items—seeds, tools and cows are common examples—are the central focus of this oft repeated tale. It goes that someone in the village, either a man or a woman, is desperately poor and destitute. Yet, even though he is of very meager means, he shares what little he has with a Fairy who is passing by his door. Unlike the stories above, the Fairy in this story is disguised and not identified until after this sharing occurs. For the human's small kindness, a gift is bestowed. It might be magical seeds, as in the tale about a boy named Jack and a beanstalk; or it could be a tool, as in the story of a miller's wheel that worked on its own to grind more grain than any other wheel in the country; or it might be a magical cow that always had milk to give and always bore the biggest and strongest calves.

The result of this magical item, whatever the item may be, is that the poor unfortunate becomes a prosperous and powerful person in his village. People from miles around come to visit the newest affluent member of society just to see the magical item. Like most other Fairy tales, this one ends sadly when the human commits a sinful error, such as greed or ungratefulness.

The human in the magical cow story decided to butcher the cow when the cow became old, thinking to reap one more benefit from her in her meat for the table. This angers the Fairy who originally bestowed the gift. The Fairy returns and rescues the cow and all of her offspring, leaving the human once again poor and without means.

The main character of this story can be either a man or a woman and is really quite a common person. He does not appear to be simple, ugly or mean-spirited. In fact he seems to be so much like any of his neighbors that you would never notice him as being special or outstanding. This may be the very reason this story has been repeated for so long, because it explains why one man in a village somehow prospers over those who are exactly like him. This could never have happened because he worked a little harder, worked longer hours, sacrificed small luxuries to invest in his farm or learned his trade a little better than all the rest. No, it clearly was because a Fairy gave him a magical gift. Had the Fairy gifted his neighbors, it would have been they, and not he, who succeeded in the village.

The evolving tales of Fairies

We are fortunate today to have copies of these Fairy legends. By the early 1700s, Fairy tales had become unpopular and were deemed to be the prattling of uneducated peasants. As the Christian church began to expand its influence in the western world, its clergy condemned the stories of Fairies because they spoke of spiritual beings and magical happenings that did not appear in the Bible; therefore, either the Fairies did not exist or they were minions of the devil. For any person to believe in the old stories or pass them on by telling them meant that he was going against the teachings of his Christian faith.

By the mid-1700s, it was the stories of the Bible that were told in the evening's firelight instead of Fairy tales, which were nearly forgotten. It would be one hundred years later, during the Victorian era, when Fairy tales would once again become popular and experience a revival in their telling.

The missing element

From the oldest of Fairy stories we learn not only how a Fairy might appear but also how he affects the lives of the humans he encounters. This research provides a basis for the artist to begin formulating interactive scenes using the Fairy as the focal point. But is it enough to truly create an accurate representation of this magical people?

For all of the descriptive notes I had at hand at this point in my research, there still seemed to be something I had missed in trying to describe a Fairy for the artist. What didn't I find? What was I searching for that does not appear in the oldest of tales? Something very obvious was missing and nagging relentlessly in my mind. Finally I realized what was not written. Old Fairies did not have wings!

Nowhere in the oldest stories of Fairies are wings mentioned. They look like miniature people, they ride horses, they have homes and families, they love music and dance, they have a wide range of emotions and they are even documented to be magical. Yet nowhere was there a descrip-

tion of a Fairy having wings or the ability to fly. Even the dictionary defines a Fairy as a diminutive, mischievous human-like being with magical powers, but it does not mention wings. At that moment I had a terrible ache in the pit of my stomach at the realization that I had no notes, no references, not even a hint from the oldest of written legends that Fairies ever had wings.

"No!" my inner child was screaming at me at the top of her lungs. "This cannot be possible." Everyone knows that Fairies have wings. It is one of our few absolute truths in this troubled world. Ask anyone, from the smallest child looking through his first picture books to the oldest sage passing on his tales to a younger generation, to describe a Fairy. The first thing he will tell you is that Fairies have wings, just like a butterfly or a bee.

So back to the piles of books at my feet I went. I made a mad dash to the library to search again through the encyclopedias of mythology and lore. I booted up the computer to start a search string under "Fairy Wings." All because somewhere in

Sunrise, pattern on page 107

© Lora S. Irish

some story I must have overlooked the clear, definitive statement that Fairies are winged creatures.

Finally, I found myself holding a Victorian era story that I remembered from my childhood. It was right there in my piles of notes, but I hadn't reread it because I already "knew" the tale; it was one of my childhood favorites. Here, in Hans Christian Andersen's tale of Thumbelina, I found the reference that seems to give Fairies wings and so changed the artist's portrayal of Fairies for the generations to come. Of course, Fairy tales and Fairy folk appear across the globe. Every country seems to have its own version of this tiny spiritual being. So there may be other references to winged Fairies that I haven't found, since it would take a lifetime to read each and every one. There may well be tales that predate Andersen's work. But at this writing, it seems that in 1853, with the publication of *Thumbelina*, our beloved Fairy got her wings.

A brief look at *Thumbelina* by Hans Christian Andersen, 1853

A childless woman desperately wanting a baby to love goes to a Fairy to ask for help. This Fairy gives her a special seed of the barleycorn in answer to the woman's wish in exchange for twelve shillings. When the woman plants the seed, a plant different from any in the farmer's field begins to grow. It is a tulip, and within the beautiful flower, a delicate and graceful Fairy maiden appears. The childless woman names her Thumbelina because she is no bigger than half as tall as a man's thumb.

Thumbelina enjoys a wonderful life with the woman until one night she is captured by a large, ugly, wet toad that believes Thumbelina will make a nice wife for his son. Taking her to his pond, the toad leaves Thumbelina on a water lily leaf to await her marriage. However, the fish in the pond know she will never be happy with the ugly toad's son as a husband, so they gnaw at the leaf until the stem is broken, making it into a tiny boat.

The tiny Fairy's adventure continues when a large beetle, called a cockchafer, picks her up from her leafy boat to take her to his home. He, however, releases Thumbelina, thinking that she is too ugly to be his wife. After all, she has only two legs, her waist is quite thin and she has no feelers.

Being allowed to leave, she next encounters a field mouse that offers her shelter in his home in exchange for a little housework. The field mouse decides that Thumbelina will make a wonderful wife for his friend the mole. Upon seeing this little Fairy, the mole falls right in love with her and takes her to his home. Unfortunately for our heroine, she is not in love with the mole because he is mean in temperament and keeps her from the sunshine and the fields of flowers that she loves.

Trapped in the mole's home as she awaits their marriage, Thumbelina is allowed to travel the underground passages and comes across the body of a swallow lying on the cold earth. The poor bird had fallen through a hole in the roof of the passage. Even though she knows the swallow is dead, Thumbelina still cannot bear that his body is cold, so she makes him a blanket of grass. The warmth from the blanket revives the swallow, which was just stiffened with the chill, and in repayment for her kindness he takes her from the mole's hole to his nest above a beautiful field of flowers.

Perched on a special, large white flower, Thumbelina meets a handsome Fairy man, not much taller than she, with a golden crown and delicate wings. This Fairy prince is called the Spirit of the Flowers. Knowing that Thumbelina is the most beautiful woman he has ever seen, he asks her to marry him, which she promptly does. Other Fairies—who all have wings—appear and rejoice, bringing Thumbelina wedding gifts. The greatest gift of all is a pair of beautiful wings that had belonged to a white fly. These are fastened to Thumbelina's shoulders so that she can fly from flower to flower. Of course, Thumbelina lives happily ever after with her Fairy prince.

We now know how the Fairy got her wings. She wasn't born with them; they were a wedding

Flutterby Iris, pattern on page 87

© Lora S. Irish

gift. This present, given to us by Hans Christian Andersen, has a tremendous impact on us artists who portray Fairies. Since Thumbelina's wings are from an existing insect, we are not limited to one style, shape or color of wings as we would have been had she been born with them. Because they are a gift and not an inherited physical characteristic, wings from any insect can be used to adorn our small mystical beings. From this time period forward, artists' renderings of Fairies show them with a wide variety of wing styles, with butterfly and bee wings being the most popular.

Through this same story, we also have learned how the Fairy became associated with the garden, for Thumbelina was born from a flower and her husband, the prince, was the Spirit of the Flowers. This connection makes the Fairy more a creature of nature than a being of human-like descent.

Four natural elements are present in this delightful tale. The childless woman represents the element of Fire that only humans could control. The toad is the creature of the Water, whereas the mouse and the mole are inhabitants of the Earth. Finally the cockchafer and the rescuing swallow symbolize the element of Air. Thumbelina herself becomes an Air element when her new wings free her from being earthbound.

Another major change comes to light in the story of Thumbelina. The Fairy is no longer to blame for catastrophes, neighbors disappearing in the night or the loss of prosperity in a human's existence. Thumbelina remains magical in that everyone who meets her falls instantly in love with her, wishing she were his wife. But she no longer retains the powers to simply disappear when her life becomes unbearable. Nor does she have the power to make others disappear, for she has no powers of revenge. Sold by her Fairy father for twelve shillings, kidnapped by a toad, helplessly adrift on a leaf boat, captured by a beetle, trapped in the underground passages of a mole…this little being seems more a victim than a perpetrator.

The Victorian Fairy, circa 1850–1920

Several major changes happened during this time that affect Fairy tales and Fairies. The advent of the printing press had allowed local histories to be recorded, so the original purpose of the Fairy tale no longer existed. Oral stories and tales were no longer needed to teach the younger generations about past happenings. Weekly newspapers and periodicals had become commonplace in the Victorian home.

These papers, needing articles to fill their columns, often included short stories of the time that could be read over and over again. The Victorian era stories, called "morality tales," were used to reinforce the social attitudes of the time. Yet since the Fairy tale was no longer an oral record, the authors had greater latitude in creating the characters, settings and adventures. Legends that had been passed on at the hearth over hundreds of years often changed a little with each telling, creating variations. Now, written and saved, the newer Fairy tales remained true and were used by the generations that followed as guidelines for both literature and art.

This new little creature is most often a female; the male Fairies were given subordinate roles in the stories. As seen in Thumbelina, there is a male Fairy who is noted as a prince, the Spirit of the Flowers and a leader of a troupe of flower Fairies, yet he gets little mention in the story beyond the fact that Thumbelina chose him as her husband. Andersen uses quite a few paragraphs to describe both the mouse and the mole, yet barely a few sentences are said about the Fairy prince. This is also reflected in the arts since there are few paintings or illustrations that show a Fairy as a man. Instead literature and artwork are filled with beautiful, young, winged maidens.

Of special note, the Fairy of the Victorian era is given a new set of clothing. In the oldest tales the Fairies' clothing is no different than their human neighbors'—anything from peasant rags to queenly gowns. Now the Fairy is scantily dressed in wisps of

Spring Blossoms, pattern on page 72

gossamer or no dress at all. One story tells that she "could barely endure the touch of the course fabric to her delicate skin." This is a great contrast to the human women that owned the Fairy's garden, for their fashions during this time required multiple layers of heavy clothing and the intolerable torture of the corset. The Fairy's love of bright colors still remains and often reflects the colors of her favorite flower. And she still loves to dance.

Victorian Fairies become free-spirited people who have little or no education and few goals or purposes in life. Instead they are content to spend their time flitting through the garden, sipping nectar and bathing in the lily ponds. Much more like the butterfly than the human, Fairies have little use beyond delighting anyone who might by chance see them as they dance through the flowers. They do still love their mischief and might be caught taking a few cookies or fresh strawberries from the table or messing up a child's room that the child swears to his mother was clean a few moments ago; yet they are seen as simple souls who can easily be tricked by mankind because of their insatiable curiosity.

What magic the Fairy keeps is limited to acts of kindness or protection of those she loves. She no longer bears the burden of being the revengeful spirit or the punishing passerby. The literary authors of the day handed these traits over to the brownies, the trolls and the occasional wicked elf. The Fairy and her breed have become instead "good Fairies" and are so noted with the stories about the Fairy Godmother, the Tooth Fairy and Tinkerbell.

If the Fairy does have a purpose in life, it is to grant the downtrodden human his life's desires. Wishes are granted that dramatically improve the person's existence, and magical gifts are freely given and never taken away. The Victorian Fairy tales end with "and they lived happily ever after" instead of "and they were never seen again." The Fairy has become a miniature magical heroine who is just waiting to champion humans in any plight.

Fairies of today

Fairies are still evolving. Like any mystical creature, the Fairy's role in society is ever expanding. Today the Fairy is seen as a female, with her male counterpart being either a human or an elf. The male Fairy has nearly become extinct, a long lost memory in the old stories.

Today's Fairy is powerful in the witch's arts, capable of casting small spells or veiling the eye of passersby. Her role as a Fairy Godmother has increased so that today she is seen as a guardian and a protector of those she chooses to love. She closely watches over her human charges in the tasks that fill their daily lives.

In reading some of the writing today, I sometimes wonder if she isn't the one who remembers to turn the gas off on the stove or unplug the coffeepot as we rush out of the house for another busy day's work. Surely she is the one who sits on our shoulder watching the oncoming traffic for us during rush hour as we, exhausted from our tasks, hurriedly head home to our families.

Her garments reflect the fashions of her new era, since Fairies can now be found dressed in any current style. Long, striped stockings adorn her legs, and fingerless gloves may help her ward off the morning's chill. Her dresses can be anything from little more than miniskirts to flowing, multiple-layered gowns; that is, if she wears any clothes at all. Even her choice of wings has increased to include the cast-off feathers of a robin, the beautiful leaves of autumn or the tattered-edged wings of a bat. To add to her adornment, a Fairy may even have antennae, which I can only suppose she obtained just as Thumbelina obtained her wings.

Today's Fairy is feistier than yesteryear's. More like Tinkerbell than Thumbelina, she is ready and willing to fly into the face of anything that might hurt her chosen companion, even the wickedest of the Captain Hooks he might engage. She is a liberated female no longer controlled by her father's wishes, her husband's demands or fate's whims.

Sweetly Shy, pattern on page 174

© Lora S. Irish

Although she remains seldom seen, she no longer interacts with just a few lucky souls. Today's Fairy can become just about anyone's loving guardian if her chosen human truly believes that Fairies exist and are not just imaginary children's story characters. Fairies are tiny touches of magic that we can carry in our hearts to defend against a world that is often too starkly cold with reality.

And she still loves to dance!

One last riddle

We have looked at the history of Fairies from the tales and legends of the past through today's stories. So one question remains, from where did Fairies come? There are several suggestions that show up in the tales.

The first theory is that an old woman with a large number of children heard that Jesus Christ was to pass by her door. Having long been ridiculed by her neighbors for having too many children, she did not want to be so shamed before the Son of God when he saw all of her offspring, so she hid half of her children from sight. When he had passed her home, she went to look for those that she had hidden but could find not a one. Having been denied the blessings of Christ, they turned into the first Fairies, destined to roam the earth as soulless beings.

The second theory is that if a human lived a life not quite good enough for heaven to take him but not quite bad enough for hell's fires, his soul, upon his death, would become a Fairy.

The third theory, and the one that seems most plausible to me, is that Fairies are created instantaneously when someone makes a selfless, pure wish or prayer for another person. Even though the wish or prayer may never come to pass, the deep love and concern inherent in the wish is so powerful that it must take living form. Thus a Fairy is born.

Of course, Thumbelina teaches us that Fairies are born from magical barleycorn seeds that blossom into tulips. I, personally, have little use for this theory. Being an avid gardener who loves to plant flowers that are said to attract Fairies, I have never seen or heard of such a seed.

CHAPTER THREE

FAIRY FAMILIES AND THEIR WING PATTERNS

OR *Who's who in the Fairy realm?*

Because the legend of Thumbelina shows that the Fairy can take the wings of a flying creature and attach them to her body, artists can use a wide variety of wings found in nature. Anything that can create a sail, such as leaves and feathers, can be used. An added feature to this legend is that because wings are not grown by the Fairy from birth but indeed are attached, we artists are not limited to real wings and are free to create our own wing styles for our Fairies.

The wing style that a Fairy sports often tells us of her breed. Although all Fairies seem to be of one species, they are noted as being from a particular group, determined by where they make their homes, their size or their special task in life. Today Fairies are recognized as falling into six categories: the Flower Fairy, the Forest Fairy, the Pixie, the Water Nymph, the Pagan Fairy and the Guardian Angel Fairy.

Bee wings

Bee or fly wings are classic examples of Fairy wings. **(See Figure 1.)** Often found as the wings of choice in Flower Fairy illustrations of the early 1900s, these wings are transparent with little or no coloring. The veining is done in a grayish brown with a touch of medium gray along the outer edge of the wing sail. They are the smallest of the Fairy wings, about the length of the Fairy's arm from her shoulder to her elbow.

Bees have two wings per side with the top wing being slightly larger than the bottom wing. This distinguishes a bee's wings from a fly's wings, which are similar in shape to a bee's lower wing but have only one wing per side.

Flower Fairies became popular with the story of Thumbelina and are still the most notable of the species. The Fairies in Victorian era Fairy tales used the wings of white flies to allow them to fly. Today's Fairies have expanded their wing wardrobes, choosing a wing not only to fly but also to add color to their lives.

Figure 1
Bee wings

Dragonfly wings

Figure 2
Dragonfly wings

The dragonfly's wings are longer than the bee's. They stretch from the Fairy's shoulders to at least her knee joint. (See **Figure 2.**) Some Fairies who sport dragonfly wings have wings so long that they cannot stand straight and tall unless the wing is allowed to hang over the edge of the flower petal. The wings are longer in length than they are tall. The veining is usually done in a slightly darker tone; the sail is shown either in a bi-color effect or in a sepia brown tone. For bi-color wings, consider using teal, jade or sea foam greens that are common to dragonflies. Often the accenting patterns for bi-tone wings are created using black.

This set of wings often represents the Water Nymphs, or the Water Fairies, who are found resting on lily pads or soaking their feet at the edge of a pond. Favorite companions of these little flutterbyes are the frog, the newt and the water snail. If you are searching for Water Fairies, they are easiest to find when the water lily blooms because the flower's sweet scent released into the night air attracts them. Water Nymphs make their homes in the abandoned toad holes found along a creek bank or along the edge of a lily pond.

Butterfly wings

Butterflies are favorite sources for Flower Fairy wings. (See **Figure 3.**) Their large, full sails and bright colors make them highly prized. Wings from this insect vary in size from the tiniest butterfly, less than one-half-inch long, to the giant wings of some South American varieties said to grow wings that span twelve inches. Flecking, spots and even long accent lines of differing colors decorate the butterfly and Fairy alike. A Fairy dressed in her butterfly wings will be vividly adorned for the evening's dance.

Flower Fairies, the largest of the breed, can be

Bee Wings, pattern on page 96

Luna Moth Pixie, pattern on page 167

found amongst the roadside wildflowers, gracing the open meadows and dancing through our formal gardens. It is the wildflowers that attract this little dainty, and gardeners of today often plant flowerbeds specializing in those plants that the Flower Fairy favors, including foxglove, larkspur, forget-me-nots, daisies and meadow rue. Every Flower Fairy loves the rose, whether cultured or briar wild.

Moth wings

Rivaling the butterfly wing in size variety, the moth

Figure 3
Butterfly wings

wing tends to be more discreet in its color tones and patterns. **(See Figure 4.)** These are perfect for the Forest Fairy who wishes to blend into the background of the surrounding scene. Although the same range of color hues and decorations are found in this group as in the butterfly group, the colors will be muted, using pastel tones and classic neutrals, such as caramel and cream. Basic gray and black sails are also common and are excellent for a formal affair.

The Forest Fairy is found deep within the woods, making her home at the base of an old tree or in a small cave. It is the Forest

Fairy who in old legends was reported as the wicked or evil member of the Fairy family. It is she who led the unsuspecting man into the Fairy ring dance or off the known path into disaster. Today Forest Fairies are a kindly folk that prefer their privacy and are seldom seen.

Bird Wings

Today's Fairies do not limit themselves to their mother's choices of wing styles. A modern Fairy is quite delighted with the discarded feathers

Figure 4
Moth wings

of a blue jay or a cardinal. Because feathers come in coloring far beyond black and tan, she will be able to create a wardrobe that holds a rainbow of wing patterns.

The Guardian Angel Fairy uses the full wing of a bird for herself. **(See Figure 5.)** She usually chooses the wings of a white dove; however, other bird wings with brighter coloring can be found. Her wing color choice can reflect her guardian task for the day. If her day's labor is to be secretive, the white full wings

© Lora S. Irish

Simply Daring, pattern on page 175

are used so that she can silently spill into your life unseen. However, if she needs your attention to some forgotten promise or labor, her wings will be bright and noisy. She will flutter where she will easily be noticed, catching your eye to guide you on the correct path or lead you to that lost object.

A Guardian Angel Fairy is not to be confused with a Biblical angel. The spiritual angel is said to stand as tall as, or taller than, an average human, often imposing in size and surrounded by mist or light clouds, whereas a Guardian Angel Fairy is never taller than a two-year-old child and appears wherever and whenever she wants.

Figure 5
Bird wings

Leaf Wings

Shaped much like a butterfly or moth wing, a leaf can provide a wide sail with ridged veining for

Figure 6
Leaf wings

our Fairy. **(See Figure 6.)** In celebration of the changing seasons, Fairies of today often choose leaves as their wings. Pale mint green leaves for a spring festival, deep blue-green leaves for a summer picnic and then orange, red and gold leaves for the fall harvest.

Pixies are a special breed of Fairies that are said by legend to paint the autumn leaves to their brilliant tones of gold, orange and red. The leaves they so carefully paint make perfect sets of wings for modern Pixies. The littlest of the Fairy species, Pixies find that mushroom patches make wonderful homes. Pixies are notably mischievous. They are often the cause for an unknown tickle or an untied shoelace. It is Pixies that are the cupids of the Fairy family because they love to make young men and women bump into each other so that they can meet and fall in love.

Bat Wings

Bat wings are showing up more and more in the Fairy's wardrobe of wing styles. **(See Figure 7.)** Here the full wing is used from the shoulder joint to the leading tip. The bat wing tends to be at least half the height of the Fairy to as long as the Fairy is tall. Usually she will complete her outfit by wearing a basic black gown with tattered edges and a high collar. Larger and taller Fairies may need to go to the Dragon family for wings.

Pagan Fairies have joined the family of flutterbyes as their newest members. Pagan Fairies specialize in little touches of witchcraft, which are often called women's charms and spells. Although a Pagan Fairy can be seen year-round in the vegetable garden, especially in the pumpkin patch, she also graces libraries that have old musty books as well as witchcraft and occult bookstores. Her favorite days of the year are, of course, Summer

Dragonfly Wings, pattern on page 98

Figure 7
Bat wings

Solstice and Allhallows Eve. She is a White Witch, or Good Witch, for those she chooses as her companions, but she may be tempted to cast small mischievous spells against those who have harmed her favorite person. Though she cannot turn your ex-boyfriend into a toad, she can at least cause him to get the sneezes.

Fairies can be broken down into groupings that correspond to the elements. The Flower Fairy is a representative of Air. For the element of Earth, you will look to the Forest Fairy and the Pixie. The Pagan Fairy is the Fire element. The Water Nymph or Water Fairy stands for the Water element.

© Lora S. Irish

Forest Nook, pattern on page 137

CHAPTER FOUR

CHANGING YOUR FAIRY'S POSE

OR How can I turn one Fairy pattern into a dozen?

Taking one Fairy pattern and turning it into a dozen Fairy patterns is actually easier than you think. Keep the same face, the same twist to the neck, the same slant to the back, and the same bend to the forward leg. Make subtle changes in their poses, their dress and their surroundings. Voila! You have quickly made them different.

Making a paper manikin

One of the first areas where you can make adjustments on the patterns is the position of the Fairy: how she stands, sits or flies. This may appear to be a difficult task, yet it is made quite simple and fun by creating a paper manikin.

Creating a Front-Facing Paper Manikin

Choose the Fairy that you wish to use as the basis for your new design. For this example I am using a front-facing Fairy pattern called *Firefly* that clearly shows her arms and her legs. **(See Figure 1.)**

Figure 1
Beginning pattern

This adaptation of the pattern *Firefly* is created by reversing the fairy image, then replacing the candle with a soft floral sprig in the background.

© Lora S. Irish

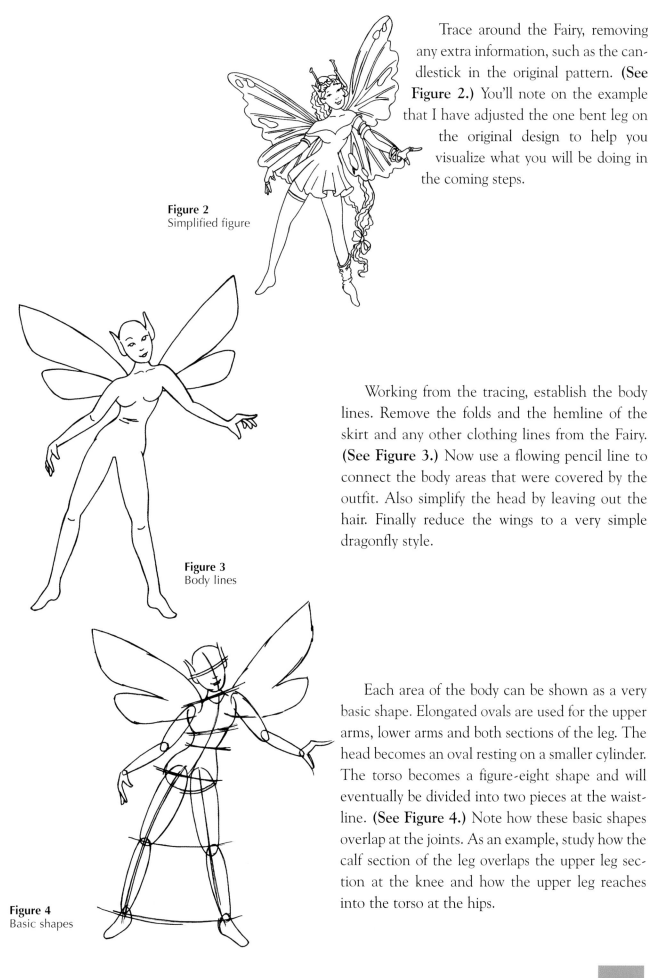

Trace around the Fairy, removing any extra information, such as the candlestick in the original pattern. **(See Figure 2.)** You'll note on the example that I have adjusted the one bent leg on the original design to help you visualize what you will be doing in the coming steps.

Figure 2
Simplified figure

Working from the tracing, establish the body lines. Remove the folds and the hemline of the skirt and any other clothing lines from the Fairy. **(See Figure 3.)** Now use a flowing pencil line to connect the body areas that were covered by the outfit. Also simplify the head by leaving out the hair. Finally reduce the wings to a very simple dragonfly style.

Figure 3
Body lines

Each area of the body can be shown as a very basic shape. Elongated ovals are used for the upper arms, lower arms and both sections of the leg. The head becomes an oval resting on a smaller cylinder. The torso becomes a figure-eight shape and will eventually be divided into two pieces at the waistline. **(See Figure 4.)** Note how these basic shapes overlap at the joints. As an example, study how the calf section of the leg overlaps the upper leg section at the knee and how the upper leg reaches into the torso at the hips.

Figure 4
Basic shapes

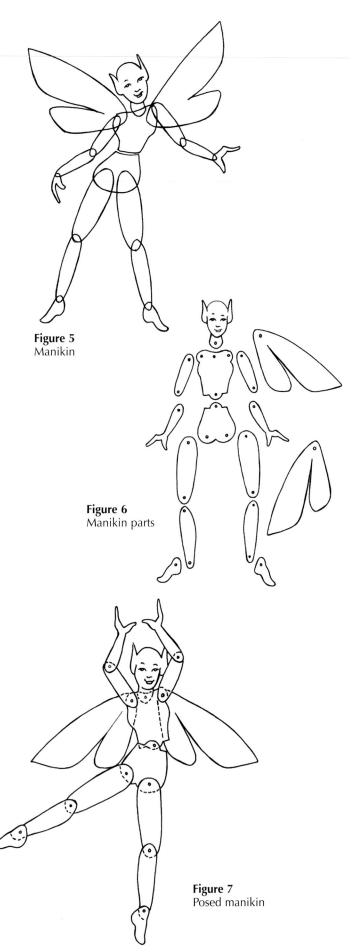

Figure 5
Manikin

Figure 6
Manikin parts

Figure 7
Posed manikin

Clean up your sketch by retracing the Fairy. **(See Figure 5.)** This will leave the working lines to create your paper manikin. Find the main body joints of your Fairy. This is where the Fairy moves: the ankles, the knees, the hips, the waist, the shoulders, the elbows, the neck and the wings. Make a pencil mark in the center of each of these overlaps. **(See Figure 6.)** When the paper manikin is cut from heavy card stock, these marks become the holes that will allow you to join the individual pieces.

On a clean sheet of tracing paper, trace around each part of the Fairy, separating each of the basic shapes. Mark where the joining holes will be. The Fairy should have a head and neck section, the two torso sections, upper arms, lower arms with hands, upper legs, lower legs, feet and wings. Note that I have added small half-circles on the two torso sections to allow these two pieces to be joined. Even though this example does not show it, the hands could have become individual manikin pieces with a joint at the wrist if you wish to bend this area.

You will need heavy card stock paper, such as a manila file folder or the cardboard from a cereal box, a glue stick, an X-Acto knife, a small hole punch and brass-plated fasteners. Use the glue stick to paste the tracing to the card stock paper. Rub the tracing paper from the center out toward the edges of the card stock to remove any bubbles or wrinkles. Allow the manikin to dry according to the glue manufacturer's instructions.

When the manikin is dry, use the X-Acto knife to cut out each section of your manikin. Use the hole punch to cut the joint marks. Overlap the appropriate body parts and join them with a brass fastener. Note on the example that the legs, arms and head are placed on top of the torso sections, whereas the wings are attached to the back. **(See Figure 7.)** Do not fold the brass fasteners too tightly; allow some room for easy movement. Cut off the excess brass tabs on the fasteners to make working with your manikin easier.

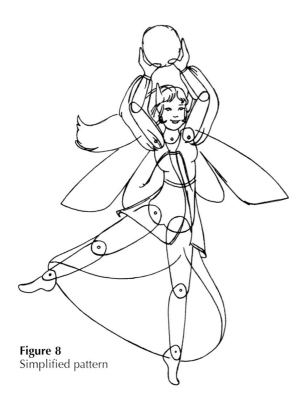

Figure 8
Simplified pattern

Now have fun playing with your manikin, moving her into all sorts of new positions and stances. When you find a new posture that you like, tighten the fasteners a little more to lock her into place. Then place your paper manikin on top of a piece of tracing paper and use a pencil to outline her. You will now have a simplified pattern of your new Fairy just like the outline we used to create the paper manikin. Clothing and hair can be sketched into place. **(See Figure 8.)**

Figure 9
Final pattern

Figure 9 shows the new Fairy with the finished detailing. Standing on the tip of one toe with one leg outstretched and arms over her head, this Fairy is in the perfect position to hold an object above her head. I chose a pentacle coin, but a flower or any other object will look just as attractive. Her name is *Pentacle Dancer*.

Paper Manikins

Using a paper manikin is a great way to try out different poses. Here are several ideas that were made from the same paper manikin.

Standing on the tip of one toe with the other leg bent implies that the Fairy's foot will rest on an object. The crossed arms imply that perhaps she is not very happy. Since Fairies hate any form of lying, the position of this paper manikin seemed just right for a Fairy that was sulking over an jar of empty promises. (*Empty Promises*, pattern on page 160)

This paper manikin is in a sitting position with her feet and bottom all at one level. I have placed her in a sitting position upon a passing turtle, where she is hitching a free ride on a hot summer's day. (*Lazy Days of Summer*, pattern on page 165)

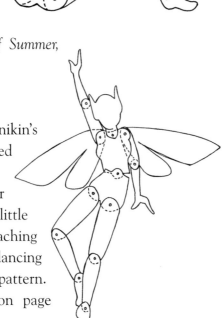

The twist to this manikin's waist and her one raised arm will make a good pattern for a dancing or flying Fairy. This lively little manikin seemed to be reaching for the stars, so a Fairy dancing on the moon is the final pattern. (*Rock 'n Roll*, pattern on page 173.)

Creating a Side-Facing Paper Manikin

To create a side-facing manikin, the steps are basically the same as those for a front-facing manikin. As an example of how to make a side-facing paper manikin, I have chosen *Sweetly Shy* because her arms and legs are very visible, making her an easy pattern to convert. **(See Figure 10.)**

Figure 10
Beginning pattern

Begin once again by reducing the pattern to just the Fairy. Then simplify her body outlines, discarding any clothing lines. **(See Figure 11.)**

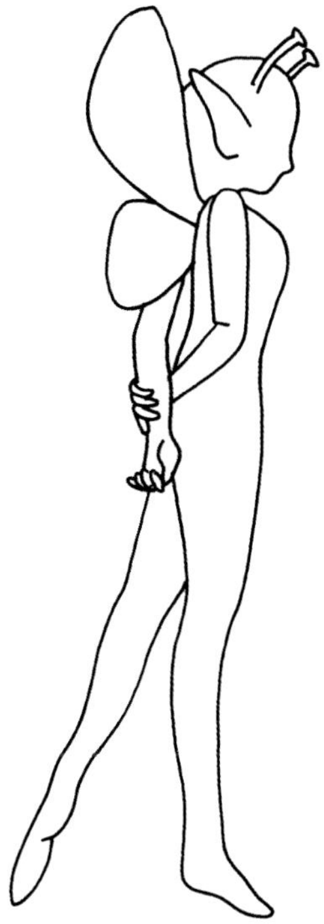

Trace around each body part to reduce each to its basic shape. Note here that I have dropped both the back leg and the back arm. **(See Figure 12.)** With a side-view manikin only one leg, one arm and one wing need to be established into the manikin's basic shape.

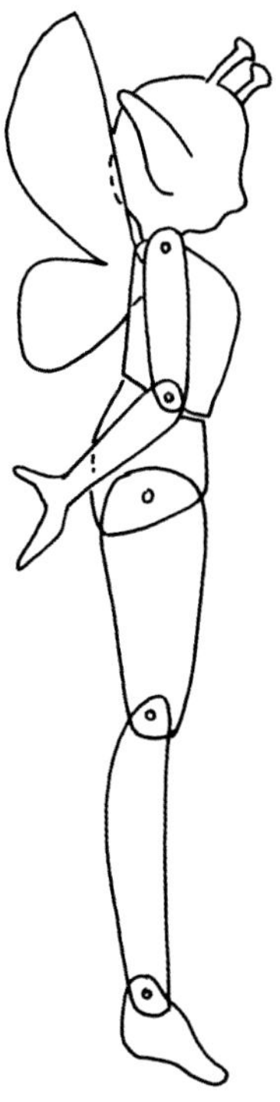

Figure 11
Body lines

Figure 12
Basic shapes

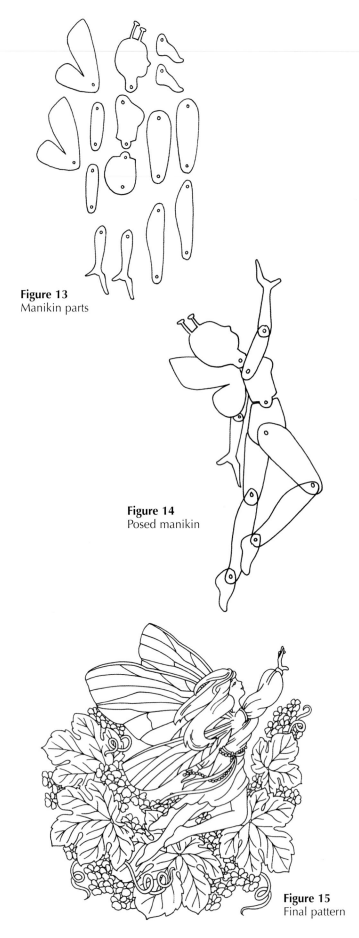

Figure 13
Manikin parts

Figure 14
Posed manikin

Figure 15
Final pattern

Make a tracing of the basic body shapes, including the joint holes. Make two copies of the arms, legs and wings. Again, if you choose, the hands may also be made into moving parts of the manikin by adding joints at the wrist. **(See Figure 13.)**

To this point, the side-facing manikin is created exactly as the front-facing manikin; however, how you attach the arms, legs and wings does change. As this manikin is a side view, one limb goes in front of the torso and the second limb goes behind the body. This holds true for the legs, the arms and the wings.

Note on the example how I have offset the legs slightly at the hips. **(See Figure 14.)** Either leg can be offset to more realistically portray how the hips twist slightly as a person moves. Usually it is the forward moving leg that is placed to the front of the torso.

There is one joint hole for the arms and wings to go through the torso. The order of the placement is one arm, the body, the wings and then the second arm. On your manikin you can leave out one of the wings to reduce the bulk in this joint. The second wing can be penciled into place when you recreate your new pattern.

Here is a finished sample of the new side-facing paper manikin Fairy. **(See Figure 15.)** With both of her legs outstretched, the tight tilt to her back and the reaching arm, she became a flying Fairy. Her name is *Flights of Fancy*.

CHAPTER FIVE

CREATING NEW WING STYLES

OR Should my Fairy have butterfly, bee, bat or dragonfly wings?

Changing the wing

Once you have your Fairy in a new position or stance, you may wish to change the size and style of wing pattern she wears. The *Evening Flutterby* pattern is an excellent design to practice wing changes because she shows both a full front wing and a three-quarter back wing. **(See Figure 1.)**

When creating new wings, it is important to note the correct placement of the upper and lower wing according to how you are viewing your Fairy. If your Fairy is viewed from the back, her upper wing lies above and slightly covers the top edge of the lower wing. For a frontal view, it will be the lower wing that is fully shown with a small part of the lower edge of the top wing being hidden behind it.

Figure 1
Existing pattern

Begin by tracing just the Fairy from the original pattern on a clean sheet of tracing paper. Discard any background scenery or information. **(See Figure 2.)**

Figure 2
Simplified wings

Using a pencil, extend the outline edges of the wings. **(See Figure 3.)** Follow the flow and curve of the existing wings. Allow the new wing edge lines to create a very large sail area with extra room for your work. You can reduce the size of the wings later.

Figure 3
Extended outlines

Section the outer wing edge into evenly divided spaces, making a pencil mark at each point. **(See Figure 4.)** This can be done visually without a ruler by first making a mark that divides the wing line in half. Next divide each of the new sections in half. Each of these quarter sections can now be divided in half. With a little practice, this division sequence done by eye can be fairly accurate and quick.

Figure 4
Wing divisions

Draw a guideline from each division point on the outer edge of the wing to the point where that wing joins the Fairy's shoulder. **(See Figure 5.)** Make these guidelines follow the natural curve of the wing sail. All these guidelines radiate from this one point in the shoulder area. Each wing, both upper and lower, will create its own curve as it flows away from her body.

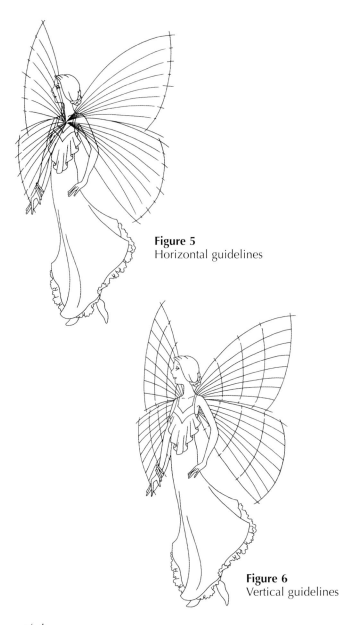

Figure 5
Horizontal guidelines

Repeat the division process for the top and the bottom edges of the wing. **(See Figure 6.)** Now mark a guideline that runs vertically through the wing sail and connects these points. Your wing should now have a graduated grid running through the sail.

Figure 6
Vertical guidelines

Use these grids as guides to insert your veining patterns and to create the flutings, tattering or scalloped finish along the outer edges of the wings. **(See Figure 7.)** Ovals and circles can be marked on the wing grids, both inside the wing to denote colored spotting or holes in the sails and outside the wing for wing tails.

Because I have created a graduated grid for both the full wing and the three-quarter wing, the markings will compliment the twist of the sail as well as ensure correct mirror image placement.

Figure 7
Detailed grid

Figure 8
New wings

Retrace the Fairy, discarding the guidelines but including the new wing outlines, veining and color spots. **(See Figure 8.)** Your Fairy is now easily adorned with a different set of sails.

Figure 9
Lilac Lassie pattern

Using common butterfly and moth wing shapes

Butterfly wings show a nice variety of edge patterns, color patterns and veining alternatives for your Fairy's new wings. This design, *Lilac Lassie*, has very simple wings with straight veining lines. Her color markings divide the wing into three vertical sections. **(See Figure 9.)** Let's use her as an example of how to alter wings.

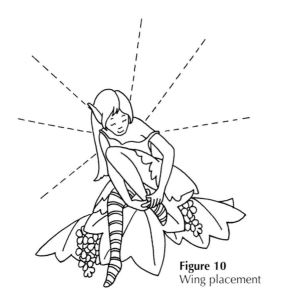

Figure 10
Wing placement

First, trace just the Fairy and a few of her leaves as the basis for experimenting with different butterfly wing styles. **(See Figure 10.)** Note that the dotted lines indicate where the new wing patterns will lie.

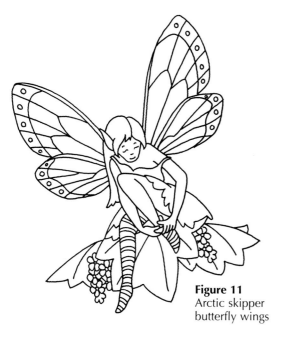

Figure 11
Arctic skipper
butterfly wings

The Arctic skipper butterfly has a general curve to the outer edge of the top wing that comes to a soft point with the upper wing vein. **(See Figure 11.)** The point in her lower wing falls about one-third of the way down the outer edge. This wing veining is sectional; the inner veins create small triangles, and the outer veins lead away from the points of those triangles. The outer edge of both the upper and the lower wing are often of a dark color with a small highlight spot of a bright hue.

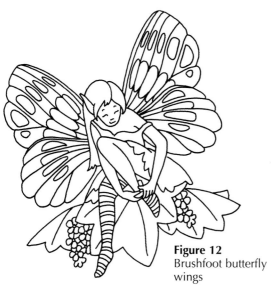

Figure 12
Brushfoot butterfly
wings

The brushfoot butterfly's wing is fluted along the edges of both the upper and the lower wing. **(See Figure 12.)** This gentle scalloping is accented with long vein lines that reach to the shoulder point of the Fairy. Large oval spots of color are contained within each of these scalloped sections.

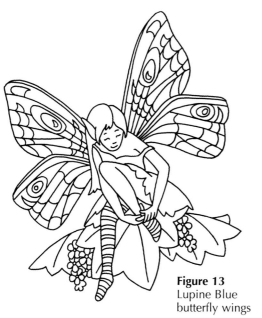

Figure 13
Lupine Blue
butterfly wings

This Fairy is decorated with the wings of a lupine blue butterfly. **(See Figure 13.)** A gentle s-curve appears along the outer edge of the upper wing. The lower wing is divided into two sections of scallops with the upper section being slightly smaller than the lower one. Just as with the brushfoot butterfly, the veins of the blue lupine's wings run the full length of the wing in long, flowing lines. The scalloped curve is carried through the coloring lines and accented with a few large circles or ovals of color.

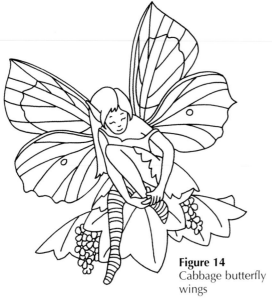

Figure 14
Cabbage butterfly
wings

The cabbage butterfly has the same gentle s-curve to her upper wing's outer edge as the blue lupine butterfly. **(See Figure 14.)** However, the lower wing shows a more randomly scalloped edge. Note that the lower wing is nearly as large as the upper wing, unlike the Arctic skipper butterfly where the lower wing is about one-half as large. The veins in the cabbage butterfly's wings radiate from two central lines with small veins branching out to the edges. The butterfly's coloring is created with one large splash of color in the center of the upper wing.

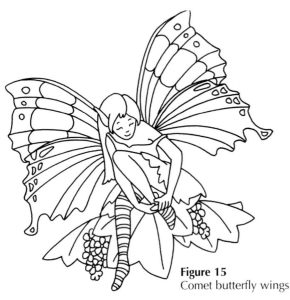

Figure 15
Comet butterfly wings

The Fairy using the comet butterfly's wings has lower sails with reversed scalloping. **(See Figure 15.)** Here the half-circles curve inward, creating gentle cut areas along the outer edge. Her lower wing also contains a small tail about two-thirds of the way down. The upper wing is just beginning to flute along the bottom third of the outer edge. A splattering of small colored flecks in the lower wings complements a large band of coloring in the upper wings.

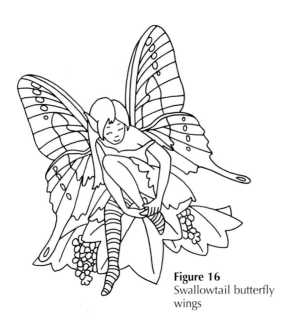

Figure 16
Swallowtail butterfly
wings

The swallowtail butterfly has a long trailing tail that sports a small spot of accent color. **(See Figure 16.)** The upper wings are much larger than the lower wings; however, it is the tail that catches your attention. The veining in a swallowtail's wing is created from two long veins that run the full length of the wing from shoulder to tip. The second, lower vein has small branches that lead off to the outer edge of the sail.

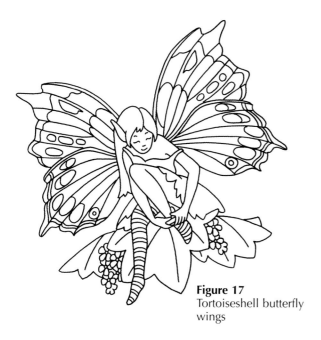

Figure 17
Tortoiseshell butterfly wings

This tortoiseshell-winged Fairy shows how fluting can be used in both the upper and the lower wing edges. **(See Figure 17.)** The wing's outer lines are a continuous series of inner, then outward, curves. Both the upper and the lower wing show a small tail area. This Fairy's coloring includes a large band of color plus colorful spots within that band, making her an excellent choice for brightly hued wing tones.

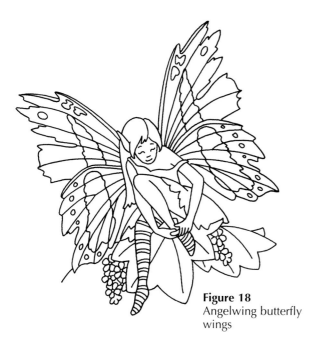

Figure 18
Angelwing butterfly wings

The satyr, or angelwing, butterfly has a ragged edge line for both wing sections. **(See Figure 18.)** In a resting position with her wings widespread, the Fairy looks just like an oak or maple leaf with numerous small points along the sail. The smooth, flowing curves of the Arctic skipper butterfly have totally disappeared for this wing style and have been replaced with a tattered and torn appearance. This butterfly carries a band of coloring through both the upper and the lower wings with a generous flecking of complementary small spots.

Lilac Lassie

Arctic Skipper

Brushfoot

Cabbage

Comet

Lupine Blue   © Lora S. Irish

Satyr-Angelwing

Swallowtail

Tortoiseshell

© Lora S. Irish

CHAPTER SIX

ALTERING YOUR FAIRY'S OUTFIT

OR How do I dress my Fairy in the best and brightest fashions?

Next in our series of possible changes for your Fairy patterns is the outfit or dress that your Fairy wears.

An outfit is an important part of any Fairy pattern because it indicates the species and the status of a particular Fairy. It is also fun to have your Fairy appropriately dressed for the scene or project that you are creating. By learning how to change her outfits, you can create anything from folk art rag doll Fairies with gingham and calico tunics sporting primitive hearts to beautifully taffeta-gowned Fairy princesses. The pattern, *Twist of Fate*, will be our model for this section of work. **(See Figure 1.)**

Figure 1
Original pattern,
Twist of Fate

A gauze skirt adds to the light and airy feeling of this fairy. The scalloped edges of her top skirt accent the tapered look of her brilliant butterfly wings.

Twist of Fate, pattern on page 177

© Lora S. Irish

Figure 2
Body lines

Figure 3
Hem guidelines

Figure 4
Basic outfit shape

Begin by simplifying your pattern, tracing only along the body lines of your Fairy. **(See Figure 2.)** Since the inner skirt on Twist of Fate is transparent and allows her legs to show, it will only be the arms between the mid-forearm and the shoulder on this pattern that you will need to create without the aid of tracing. Note the tilt to her shoulders, breast line and hips. The gridlines you establish in the next step will need to follow these body slants.

Establish the outline of the Fairy's dress, and then add a grid by dividing the dress into graduated portions by eye. **(See Figure 3.)** This system of establishing a grid is the same system we used in the previous chapter on changing a Fairy's wings.

Let's look first at the guidelines, working from the top of her shoulders down to her ankles. Along her shoulder area there are guidelines noted for a boat neck curve, a sweetheart neckline and an off-the-shoulder line. Below the breast a dashed line is marked for an Empire dress style. Next her waistline is shown, and below this are dashed guidelines for either a central panel downward v-line or the double-pointed tails of a vest. Her hemlines are shown next, with the top line marked for a mini-skirt, followed by an over-the-knee hemline, a middy hemline and, finally, a floor-length gown.

Because of the twist to her back and hips, a swaying motion is implied by the stance of this Fairy. I have tilted the cup of the skirt gridlines to reflect that implied sway. Use the inner lines along the legs to create a tightly hugging dress skirt; use the outer lines to create a full bell skirt.

Finally the hair is shown in three possible lengths. Again, because of the body twist to this Fairy, the hair will curve and flow with the skirt lines.

Pick the gridlines you'd like for your Fairy. Here I have chosen the boat neckline for her bodice top with an off-the-shoulder line for a double-pointed vest. The dress has a medium-width bell flare and a middy length. **(See Figure 4.)**

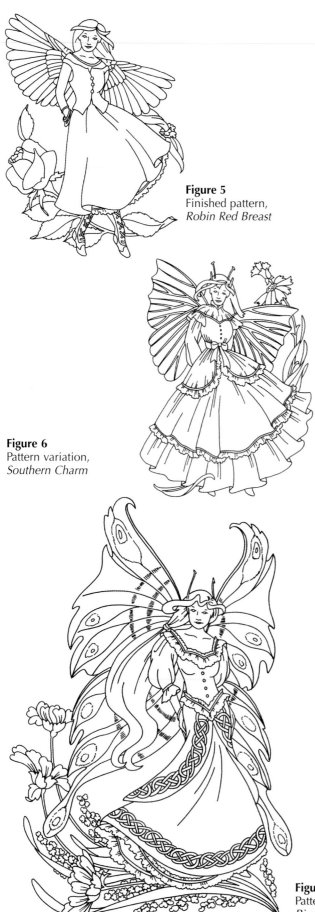

Figure 5
Finished pattern,
Robin Red Breast

Figure 6
Pattern variation,
Southern Charm

Figure 7
Pattern variation,
River Dance

Here is the finished new pattern, *Robin Red Breast*. **(See Figure 5.)** Her full middy skirt has had a few folds added, plus just a touch of petticoat appears along the hemline. Large buttons accent her vest, and it is the wings of a robin that she has chosen for today's outfit. A red rose will make a wonderful background flower for this little Fairy. A hair band adds just a little color to the end of her ponytail.

For *Southern Charm* I have again used the off-the-shoulder neckline, but this time I've defined the yoke pattern with a lacy top. **(See Figure 6.)** Her extremely full skirt begins at the waist and is divided into layers along the mini-skirt line and the middy skirt line and finally falls to a full-length gown. Lots of ruffles and lace finish off the clothing design. Because this Fairy's dress is so ornate, I have chosen simple wings that will accent, but not detract from, her new outfit.

River Dance uses the sweetheart neckline to start the top of her outfit. **(See Figure 7.)** A deep v-line bodice is highlighted with a hip accent of ruffles. Because I wished to make her appear as if she were dancing, the skirt has been flared out along the guidelines at the center portion, then back toward the opposite side at the hemline. This emphasizes the twist implied by the original posture of our Fairy. Her skirt is also created in layers with an open panel starting at the waist and reaching down to the middy skirt line. I have shortened the formal length of the skirt slightly to allow lots of petticoat ruffles surrounding her feet. A Celtic braid on the edges of the skirt and serrated butterfly wings accent her final look.

River Dance, pattern on page 171

© Lora S. Irish

Celestial Moon Pixie

Blue Celestial Moon

Blue Celestial Sun

A simple change in background and outfit can lead to an entirely new fairy design.

Celestial Sun Pixie

CHAPTER SEVEN

PLACING YOUR FAIRY IN A NEW SCENE

OR *What else can my Fairy do besides sit on flowers?*

We have explored the steps to making physical changes in your Fairy and how to give her a new outfit. Now let's look at a few ideas for new scenery and settings.

Favorite scenes and background ideas based on the legends and tales about Fairies are often either natural settings or scenes that can be found around the Fairy's home. Using the ideas in this chapter will give you guidelines for how to place Fairies in your arts and crafts. Let's look at just a few to get your imagination going.

Midnight Munchies,
pattern on page 130

Water Nymphs

A Water Nymph can be found along pond banks, sitting on lily pads, resting in lotus blossoms and accompanied by frogs, newts, dragonflies and snails. Accent items in your scenes can include cattails, water irises, daylilies and moss along the water's edge. This Fairy is often nude or holding a small bit of cloth for drying. The birdbath is another place you might find this Water Fairy. She is the Fairy associated with the Celtic knot.

Water Nymph Project Suggestions

1. Pool party invitation, beach towel accents, painted sun umbrella for the pool
2. Appliqué accents for the guest towels in the bathroom, painted aromatherapy bath candles, towel hangers
3. Anywhere around the kitchen, including on wooden spoons, menu boards, hot pads and placemats
4. Reminder clips made with scroll saw work and clothespins
5. Refrigerator magnets to hold children's artwork

Flower Fairies

A Flower Fairy is found surrounded by wildflowers and meadow blossoms; she is a sun worshiper. You will find her sitting on the edge of a flower or large leaf, sleeping in its center or hovering just above the crown of the open bloom. Consider using her with bouquets and sprays of flowers, fruit tree branches in blossom and potted spring bulbs. The Flower Fairy's companions are butterflies, bees and grasshoppers.

Flower Fairy Project Suggestions

1. Tole painting on clay flowerpots, wooden jewelry boxes and bread board signs
2. Door wreaths and wall basket arrangements
3. Stained-glass window sun catchers
4. Birth announcements and birthday party invitations
5. Diary ornaments and memory book accents

Orange Marmalade,
pattern on page 102

Forest Fairies

It is the dark floor of the woods that attracts the Forest Fairy. Her scenes may include piles of fallen leaves, acorns, walnuts, Indian pipe fungus, May apples and old tree roots. The half shell of a walnut is her favorite place to sleep. She is the babysitter of the Fairy family, so she may be found perching on the edge of a nest or sitting on a telephone line where the blackbirds light. Mice, wood snails and chipmunks are her next-door neighbors. Mouse holes, piles of fallen branches and knotholes in trees make excellent houses.

Forest Fairy Project Suggestions

1. Autumn dried flower arrangements, wreath door hangers
2. Accent to bird nest wall hangings
3. Pillows for a dark, quiet den or retreat within your home, sofa throws and quilted wall hangings
4. Do Not Disturb signs for a child's door handle
5. Christmas tree ornaments and snow Fairy rag dolls

Orange Marmalade, pattern on page 102

© Lora S. Irish

The Babysitter,
pattern on page 108

Pixies or Mushroom Fairies

The Pixie, or Mushroom Fairy, often is found living inside a discarded work boot, at the bottom of an old tin can or under the front step of your home. While the Flower Fairy and Forest Fairy enjoy the rural setting, this vixen is our country girl. She is most often found near a mushroom patch, but she also frequents the farmyard, having a liking for the calves, lambs, puppies and, of course, kittens. Being so small, if she decides to take up living within your home, she might use a sewing thimble or the folds of your pillowcase for a bed. Snails make excellent pets for this Fairy, as do crickets, babies of any type and small moths. She is the party animal of the species and the mischief-maker.

Pixie Project Suggestions

1. Clean Your Room sticky notes, homemade calendars, accents for your appointment book or address book covers
2. You're Invited party invitations, bridal shower accents and baby shower gifts
3. Folk art rag dolls, tee-shirt paintings and appliqués for clothes bags and children's sweatshirts

4. Wooden stakes along a walkway or driveway, scroll saw name plaques
5. Accents for arts and crafts totes, crafts apron appliqué

Pagan Fairies

It is the Pagan Fairy that enjoys the family garden plot, whether it is an acre wide farm plot or a small tomato planter. She is the one who carried the magic seeds of the old lore and today has a green thumb with your houseplants, especially African violets and hanging baskets of bird nest ferns. This Fairy even enjoys city living and can be found happily camped in your patio garden or in the bookshelves of the local library where she frequents the oldest leather-bound editions of mythology. Any type of school is of interest to the Pagan Fairy, and she may be tempted to hitch a ride in your kindergartener's backpack just to visit an academic setting.

Pagan Fairy Project Suggestions

1. Tags for homemade jellies and jams, labels for your favorite dill pickle recipe or cookies-in-a-jar gift
2. Gift baskets using seeds and gardening tools, fruit basket tags and cookie plate covers
3. Scrapbook adornments and bookmarkers
4. Accents for school clothes, book covers and backpacks, Reading Can Be Fun signs for the library or schoolroom
5. Painted garden row markers and plant tags

Pixie Perch,
pattern on page 132

CHAPTER EIGHT

PATTERNS

T o get you started in Fairy art, I have provided nearly 100 patterns for your use. On the following pages, you will find Storybook Fairies, Mushroom Pixies, Modern Pagan Fairies, Old Folk Tale Fairy Princesses, lots of Flower Fairies and even a few Guardian Angel Fairies. As you browse through the designs, remember that Fairies come in all sorts of shapes and sizes, from the tiniest of the breed, the Mushroom Fairy, to the Pagan Fairy that stands as tall as a leather-bound book of spells. Your Fairy can have any color of skin, any shade of hair and a rainbow for her clothing palette. Her wings can be gifted from a butterfly, created from leaves or even fashioned from the lost feather of a bird. Colors abound when you choose a Fairy design.

As an artist, I have tried to provide a large selection of Fairies in a wide number of backgrounds, scenes and situations. However, there is always a pattern in any arts and crafts book that would be "just perfect if only…." Perhaps you will fall in love with one Fairy pattern but wish that there were a design for the same Fairy in a different situation or with a different set of wings. You might wish to use the wings, face and position of a classical Fairy but would rather have her dressed in modern clothing. Now that you have worked your way through the information on the preceding pages, these changes can be easily made.

© Lora S. Irish

© Lora S. Irish

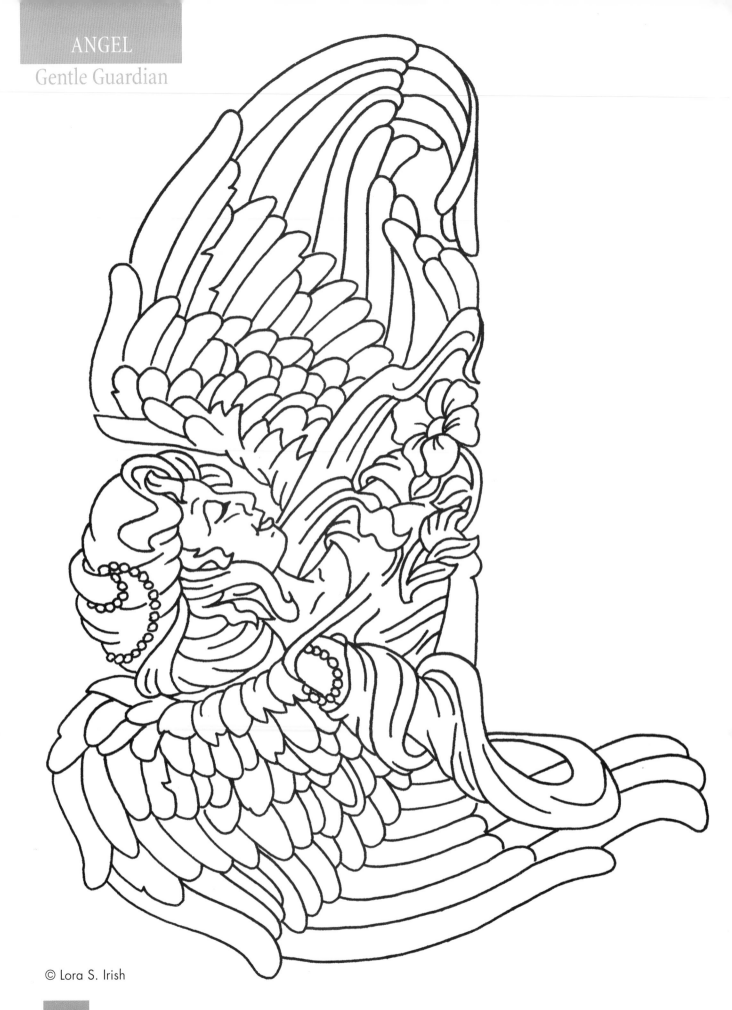

© Lora S. Irish

© Lora S. Irish

© Lora S. Irish

© Lora S. Irish

© Lora S. Irish

© Lora S. Irish

© Lora S. Irish

© Lora S. Irish

© Lora S. Irish

© Lora S. Irish

© Lora S. Irish

© Lora S. Irish

© Lora S. Irish

© Lora S. Irish

© Lora S. Irish

© Lora S. Irish

© Lora S. Irish

© Lora S. Irish

© Lora S. Irish

© Lora S. Irish

© Lora S. Irish

© Lora S. Irish

© Lora S. Irish

© Lora S. Irish

© Lora S. Irish

© Lora S. Irish

© Lora S. Irish

© Lora S. Irish

© Lora S. Irish

© Lora S. Irish

OAK
GOLD

MAPLE
RED

© Lora S. Irish

© Lora S. Irish

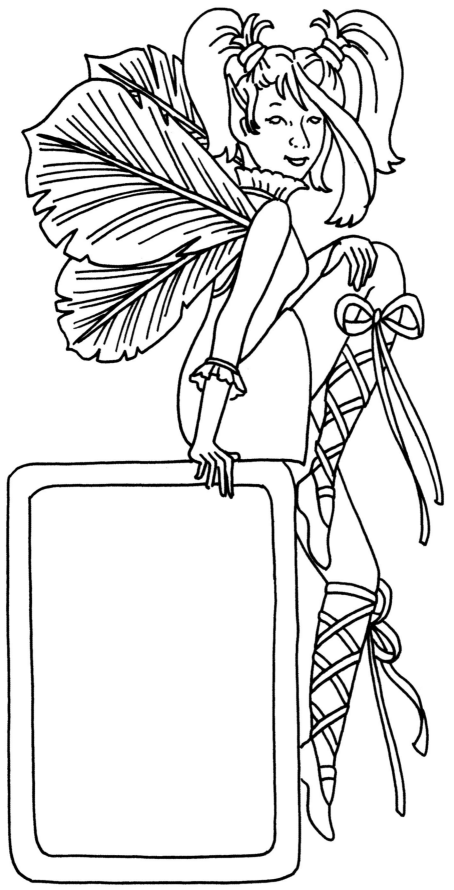

© Lora S. Irish

© Lora S. Irish

© Lora S. Irish

© Lora S. Irish

© Lora S. Irish

© Lora S. Irish

© Lora S. Irish

© Lora S. Irish

© Lora S. Irish

© Lora S. Irish

© Lora S. Irish

© Lora S. Irish

© Lora S. Irish

© Lora S. Irish

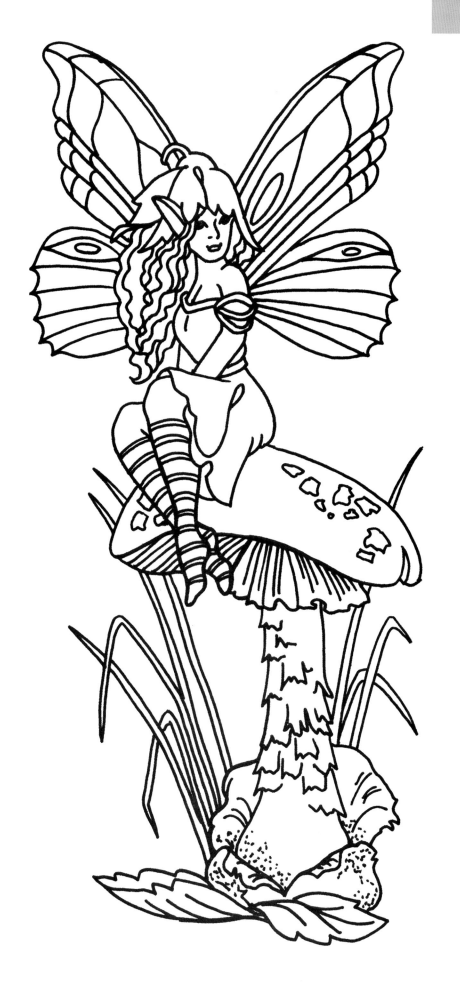

© Lora S. Irish

© Lora S. Irish

© Lora S. Irish

© Lora S. Irish

© Lora S. Irish

© Lora S. Irish

© Lora S. Irish

© Lora S. Irish

© Lora S. Irish

© Lora S. Irish

© Lora S. Irish

© Lora S. Irish

© Lora S. Irish

© Lora S. Irish

© Lora S. Irish

© Lora S. Irish

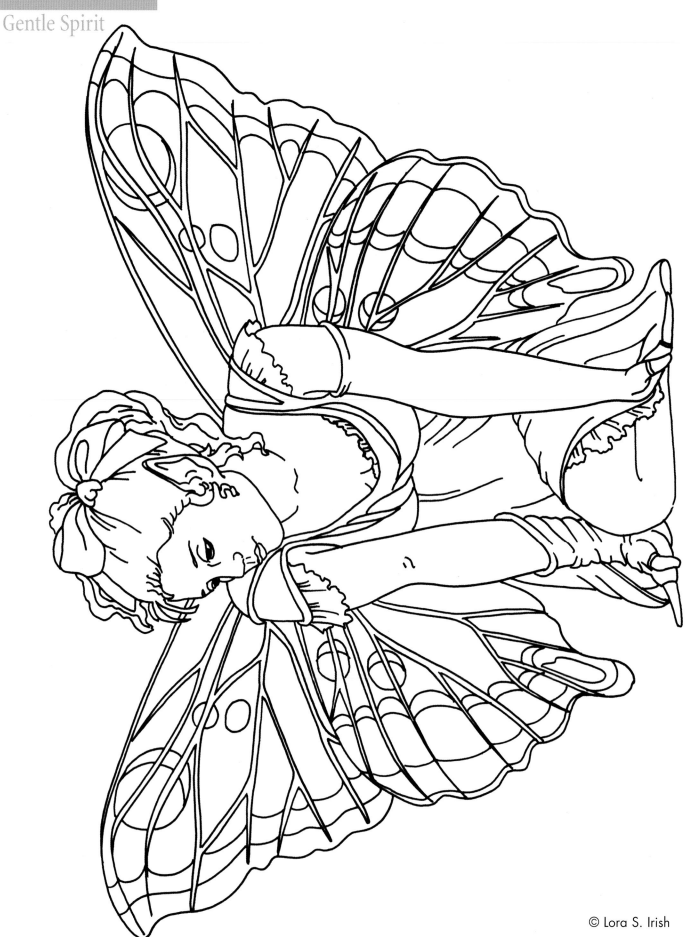

© Lora S. Irish

© Lora S. Irish

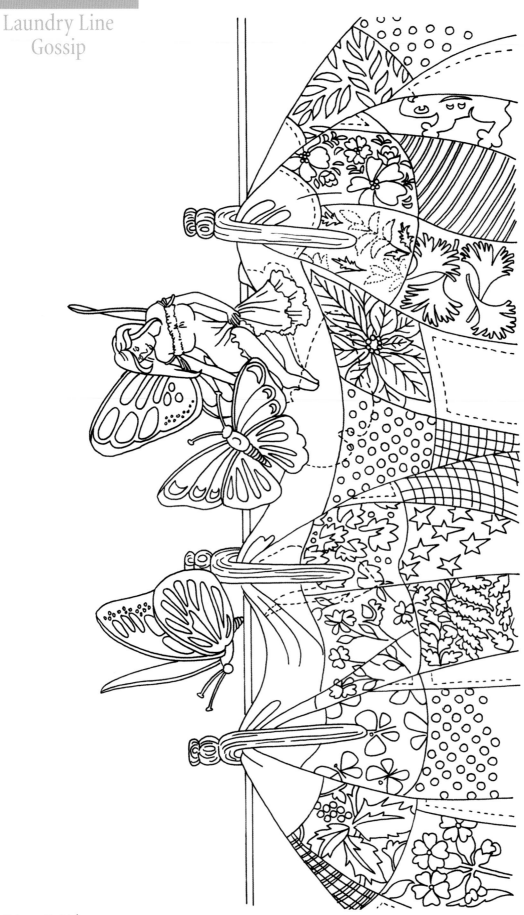

© Lora S. Irish

© Lora S. Irish

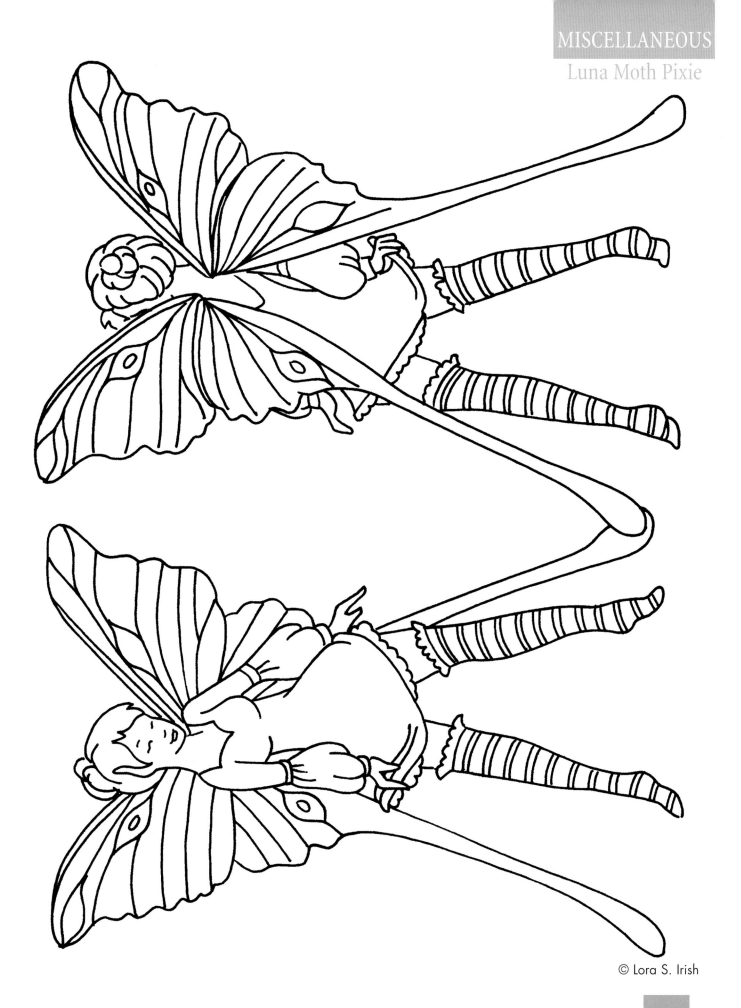

© Lora S. Irish

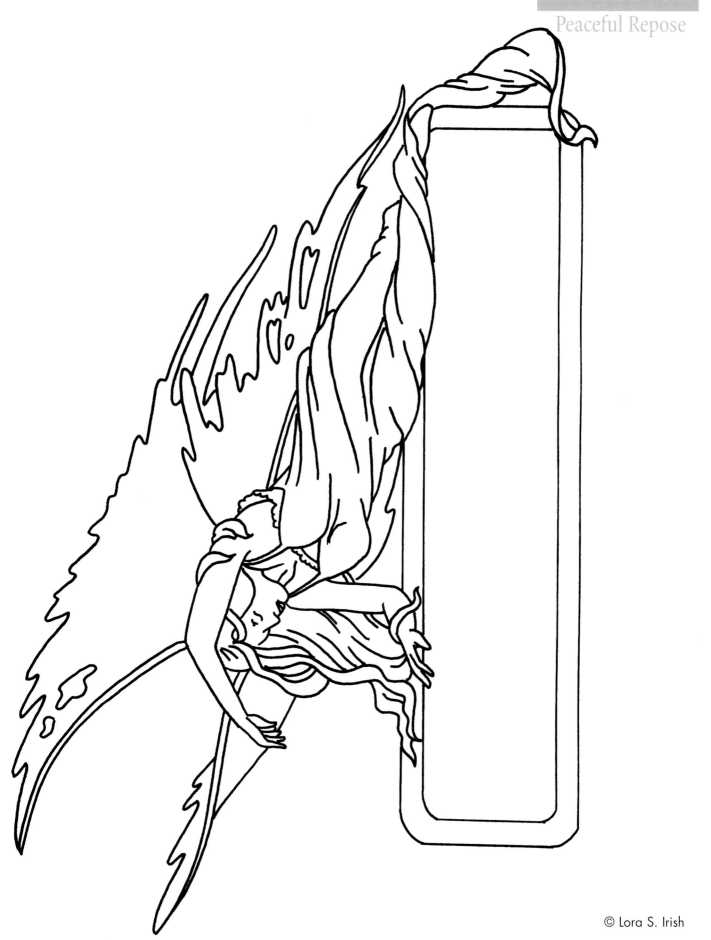

© Lora S. Irish

© Lora S. Irish

© Lora S. Irish

© Lora S. Irish

© Lora S. Irish

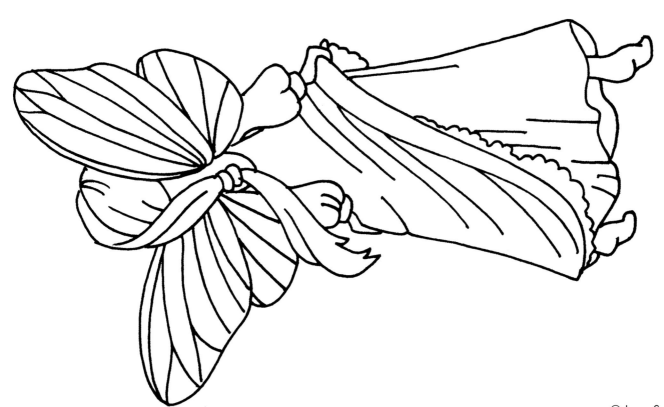

© Lora S. Irish

© Lora S. Irish

© Lora S. Irish

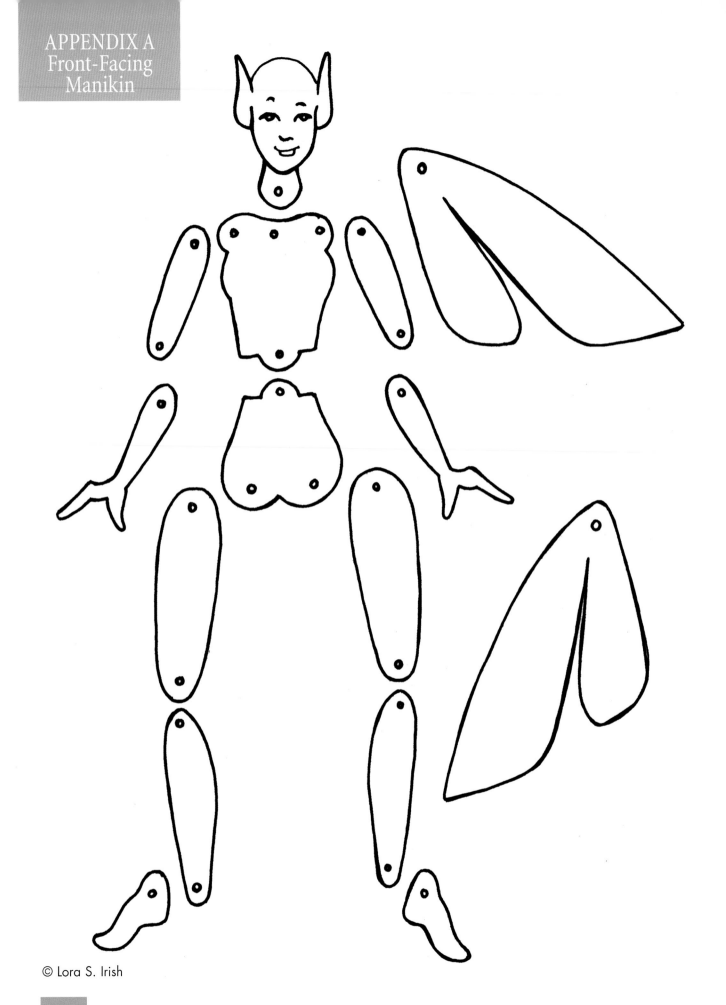

© Lora S. Irish

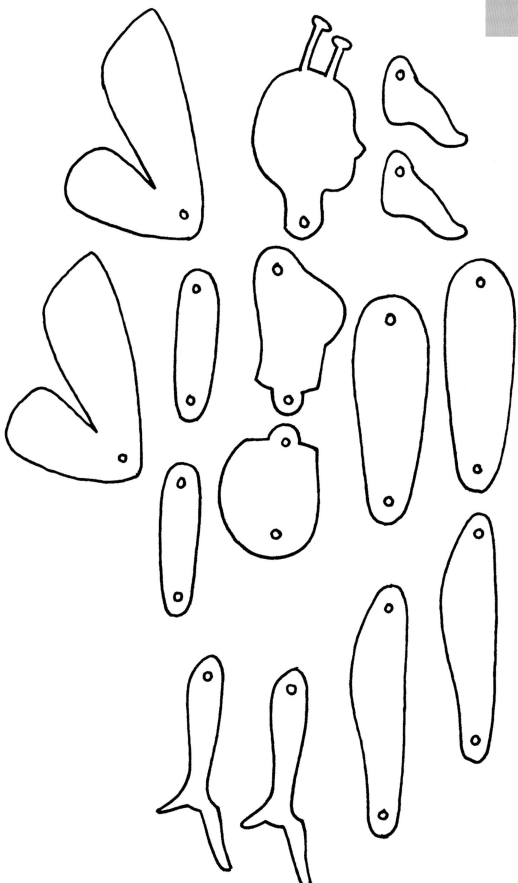

© Lora S. Irish

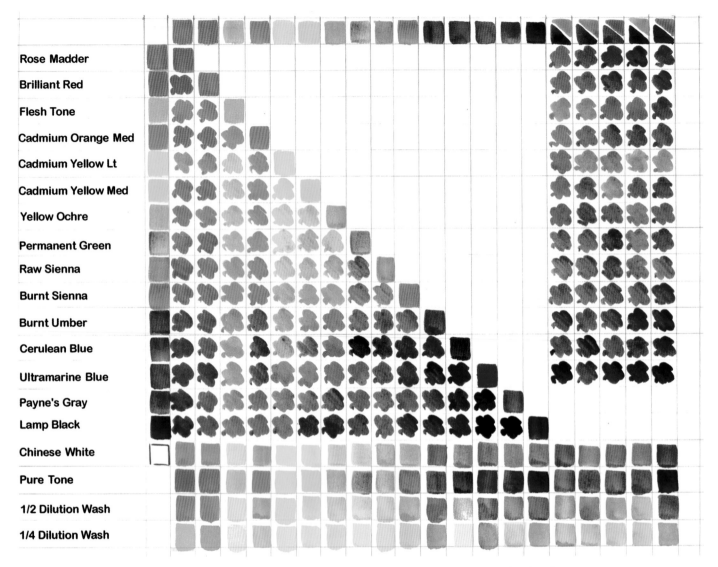

| | Rose Madder |
| Brilliant Red |
| Flesh Tone |
| Cadmium Orange Med |
| Cadmium Yellow Lt |
| Cadmium Yellow Med |
| Yellow Ochre |
| Permanent Green |
| Raw Sienna |
| Burnt Sienna |
| Burnt Umber |
| Cerulean Blue |
| Ultramarine Blue |
| Payne's Gray |
| Lamp Black |
| Chinese White |
| Pure Tone |
| 1/2 Dilution Wash |
| 1/4 Dilution Wash |

Picking the colors that you will use on a craft or art project can decide the visual impact that the finished project will have. Creating a reference chart from the colors in your palette and the possible mixtures made from those colors can make choosing your color combinations easier. This is also a great way for you, the artist, to discover the wonderful color mixes your paint box contains.

This color chart is created using watercolors, but it can be made the same way with oil or acrylic paints. Color charts are worked in three sections: the first for pure color mixed with pure color, the second for diluted colors, and the third for shading tones. In this sample the first section is created with the first 15 vertical spots and the first 15 horizontal spots along the vertical and horizontal axis. Each pure color in this section is mixed with a second pure color. The second section lies below this main grouping and is represented in the last five horizontal rows where each pure color is mixed with either white or diluted with water to produce thinned washes of the pure color. The third section lies to the far right of the main chart using the vertical rows numbered 1 through 5. Here each color will be mixed with a shading mixture of two colors to create muted tones of the pure color.

Each color that you use will be worked through two different rows on the chart. One row will be a horizontal row starting where the color's name appears on the vertical column. The second row is worked vertically from where that same color appears in the top horizontal row. So each color will be worked in one row left to right across the chart and in one row up and down across the chart.

After the chart is complete you can use it to choose colors that will complement your painting. Pick one of the color mixes, then check what two colors were used to create it by following the row left to a pure color on the vertical column and down to a pure color on the horizontal row.

To create the colors of the main section on the chart, each pure color on the named vertical row is mixed one part to one part with the pure color on the horizontal row. For example, find Yellow Ochre on the named vertical row. The color mixes for Yellow Ochre are worked along its corresponding horizontal row. Yellow Ochre is painted, unmixed with any other color, into the first grid of this horizontal row. You can tell this is a pure color because it is painted in that grid as a square. Then Yellow Ochre is mixed half and half with Rose Madder for the second grid, Brilliant Red for the third, Flesh Tone for the fourth, Cadmium Orange for the fifth, Cadmium Yellow Light for the sixth, and Cadmium Yellow Medium for the seventh grid. Each of these mixes is shown as a brush stroke in its grid. The eighth grid has returned to Yellow Ochre along the top vertical row and so is painted unmixed and in a square. Once the pure color along the top horizontal row is reached, the painting stops. Any other grids along that row would be repeated mixes.

Once the color mixes for one color are finished on the main section, the mixes for the diluted section at the bottom of the chart are next. Because I created this color chart using watercolors, I used water for the diluting media. Acrylic colors would be thinned with water; oils would be diluted with turpentine. The first horizontal row of this section shows me what the color will look like when mixed with white to create a pastel shade. The next three horizontal rows show the color as a progressively thinner wash. This section is worked top to bottom from the main color's position on the top horizontal row down through the grids on its vertical column. For example, if you find the Yellow Ochre square along the top horizontal row then run your finger down that row to the dilution section, you'll discover its color when mixed with white and when thinned to a wash.

The third section of the color chart is the shading section. It is worked left to right along the color's horizontal row. This area is worked just like the main section: Mix one part pure color to one part of the shadow mix for that row. The shadow mixes, listed by number in the white triangle of the main section, are mixed one part to one part. As an example, the first shadow grid for Yellow Ochre will first be mixed one part Yellow Ochre with one part of a half-and-half mixture of Yellow Ochre and Lamp Black. By creating shadow mixes you can increase the muted and neutral tones in your painting palette well beyond the range made by using just dark brown or black.

Having completed my chart using fifteen pure colors, I now discover that, in a half-and-half mixture rate, my paint palette can create 15 pure colors, 105 pure color mixes, 65 shadow mixes, and 60 pastels and washes. This gives me a much greater range of choices then my original fifteen colors straight from my paint box. You can increase this color chart by including one-part-to-two-part mixes and one-part-to-three-part mixes for those particular colors. As an example, Rose Madder seems to always be part of my paint palette. By extending this chart for Rose Madder, I see an even greater range of possibilities for using this color.

Pattern Index

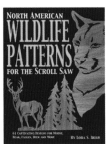

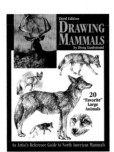